PROLOGUE

In this village, when the ripened ears of wheat sway in the breeze, it is said that a wolf runs through them.

This is because one can make out the form of a running wolf in the shifting stalks of the wheat fields.

When the wind is too strong and the stalks are blown over, it is said that the wolf has trampled them. When the harvest is poor, it is said that the wolf has eaten it.

It was a nice turn of phrase, but it had a troublesome aspect that flawed it, she felt.

Still, lately it was a popular sort of expression, and there were few remaining who wielded it with the sort of familiarity or awe it had held in the past.

Although the autumn sky that was visible between the swaying stalks of wheat had not changed in hundreds of years, conditions below that sky had indeed changed.

The villagers who tended the wheat as the years passed lived for seventy years at the most.

Perhaps it would be worse for them to go centuries without changing.

Maybe that is why there is no need for them to honor the ancient agreement, *she thought.*

In any case, she knew she no longer had a place here.

The mountains that rose in the east caused the clouds over the village to drift mostly north.

She thought of her homeland beyond those drifting clouds and sighed.

Returning her gaze from the sky to the fields, her eyes fell upon her magnificent tail, which twitched just past her nose.

With nothing better to do, she set to grooming it.

The autumn sky was high and clear.

Harvest time had come again.

Many wolves were running through the wheat fields.

CHAPTER ONE

"So that's the last, then?"

"Hm, looks like . . . seventy pelts, on the nose. Always a pleasure."

"Hey, anytime. You're the only one who'll come this far into the mountains, Lawrence. I should be thanking *you*."

"Ah, but for my trouble I get truly fine pelts. I'll come again."

The usual pleasantries concluded, Lawrence managed to leave the village just around five o'clock. The sun was just beginning its climb when he left, and it was midday by the time he descended from the mountains and entered the plains.

The weather was good; there was no wind. It was a perfect day for dozing in the wagon as he crossed the plains. It seemed absurd that only recently he had felt the chill of the approaching winter.

This was Lawrence's seventh year as a traveling merchant, and his twenty-fifth since birth. He gave a huge yawn in the driver's box.

There were few grasses or trees of any notable height, so he had an expansive view. At the very edge of his field of vision, he could see a monastery that had been built some years earlier.

He didn't know what young noble was cloistered in this remote location. The masonry of the building was magnificent, and unbelievably it even had an iron gate. Lawrence seemed to remember that roughly twenty monks lived there, attended to by a similar number of manservants.

When the monastery had first been built, Lawrence had anticipated fresh clientele; the monks were somehow able to secure supplies without employing independent merchants, though, so his dreams were fleeting.

Admittedly the monks lived simply, tilling their fields, so trade with them would not be especially profitable. There was another problem in that they would probably solicit donations and leave their bills unpaid.

As far as simple trade went, they were worse partners than out-and-out thieves. Still, there were times when trade with them was convenient.

Thus Lawrence looked in the direction of the monastery with some small regret, but then his eyes narrowed.

From the direction of the monastery, someone was waving at him.

"What's this?"

The figure did not look like a manservant. They wore dark brown work clothes. The waving figure was covered in gray clothing. His deliberate approach likely meant some hassle, but ignoring him could make matters worse later. Lawrence reluctantly turned his horse toward the figure.

Perhaps having realized that Lawrence was now headed his way, the figure stopped waving but made no move to approach. He appeared to be waiting for the cart's arrival. It would hardly be the first time that a Church-associated person demonstrated arrogance. Lawrence was in no mood to take every such insult personally.

As he approached the monastery and the figure became clearer, Lawrence muttered in spite of himself:

". . . a knight?"

He at first dismissed the idea as ridiculous, but as he drew nearer he saw that it was unmistakably a knight. The gray clothing was in fact silver armor.

"You, there! What's your business here?"

The distance between them was still too far for conversation, which is why the knight yelled. He apparently felt no need to introduce himself, as if his position were obvious.

"I am Lawrence, a traveling merchant. Do you require my service?"

The monastery was now directly in front of him. He was close enough to count the number of servants working in the fields to the south.

He also noted that the knight in front of him was not alone. There was another one past the monastery, perhaps standing guard.

"A merchant? There's no town in the direction you came from, merchant," said the knight haughtily, sticking out his chest as if to display the golden cross that was engraved there.

But the mantle draped over his shoulders was gray, indicating a knight of low rank. His blond hair looked freshly cut, and his body did not look as if it had been though many battles; so his pride most likely came from being a new knight. It was important to deal with such men carefully. They tended to be excitable.

So instead of replying, Lawrence took a leather pouch out of his breast pocket and slowly undid the twine that held it closed. Inside were candies made of crystallized honey. He plucked one out and popped it in his mouth, then offered the open bag to the knight.

"Care for one?"

"Mmm," said the knight, hesitating momentarily before his desire for the sweet candy won out.

Still, perhaps because of his position as a knight, a considerable amount of time passed between his initial nod and when he actually reached out and took a honey drop.

"A half-day's travel east of here there's a small village in the mountains. I was trading salt there."

"Ah. I see you've a load in your cart. Salt as well?"

"No, but furs. Look," said Lawrence, turning around and removing the tarp that covered his load, revealing a bundle of magnificent marten pelts. A year's salary of the knight before him was paltry compared with its worth.

"Mm. And this?"

"Ah, this is wheat I received from the village."

The sheaf of wheat in the corner of the mountain of furs had been harvested in the village where Lawrence had traded his salt. It was hardy in cold weather and resisted insects. He planned to sell it in the northwest, where crops had sustained heavy frost damage.

"Hm. Very well. You may pass."

It was a strange way of speaking for someone who'd summoned him over so high-handedly earlier, but if Lawrence were to meekly say, "Yes, sir," now, a fine merchant he'd be.

"So, what occasions your post here, sir knight?"

The knight's brow knitted in consternation at the question and furrowed still deeper as he glanced at the bag of honey drops.

He was well and truly caught now. Lawrence undid the bag's string closure and plucked out another sweet, giving it to the knight.

"Mmm. Delicious. I should thank you."

The knight was being reasonable. Lawrence inclined his head gratefully, using his best trader's smile.

"The monks have caught wind of a big pagan festival that's approaching. Thus the increased guard. Do you know anything of this festival?"

If his face had betrayed any hint of his disappointment at the explanation, calling it a third-rate performance would have been generous. So Lawrence only affected a pained expression and answered, "Sadly, I know nothing." This was of course a huge lie, but the knight was just as mistaken, so there was nothing for it.

"Perhaps it truly is being held in secret, then. Pagans are a cowardly lot, after all." The knight was so mistaken it was amusing, but Lawrence merely agreed and took his leave.

The knight nodded and thanked him again for the honey drops.

Undoubtedly they had been delicious. Most of a knight's money went to equipment and lodging; even an apprentice cobbler lived a better life. It had surely been a long time since the knight had eaten anything sweet.

Not that Lawrence had any intention of giving him another piece.

"Still, a pagan festival, they say?" Lawrence repeated the knight's words to himself once the monastery was well behind him.

Lawrence had an inkling of what the knight was talking about. Actually, anyone from this area would know about it.

But it was no "pagan festival." For one thing, true pagans were farther north, or farther east.

The festival that happened here was hardly something one needed knights to guard against.

It was a simple harvest festival, of the sort to be found nearly anywhere.

True, this area's festival was somewhat grander than the typical celebration, which is probably why the monastery was keeping an eye on it and reporting to the city. The Church had long been unable to keep control over the area, which undoubtedly made it all the more nervous about goings-on.

Indeed, the Church had been eager to hold inquisitions and convert heathens, and clashes between natural philosophers and theologians in the city were far from rare. The time when the Church could command the populace's unconditional submission was vanishing.

The dignity of the institution was beginning to crumble — even if the inhabitants of the cities said nothing, all were gradually beginning to realize it. In fact, the pope had recently had to petition the monarchs of several nations for funds when tithes had come in below expectations. Such a tale would have been preposterous even ten years before.

Thus the Church was desperate to regain its authority.

"Business everywhere will suffer," said Lawrence with a rueful smile, popping another honey drop into his mouth.

The western skies were a more beautiful golden hue than the wheat in the fields by the time Lawrence arrived in the plains. Distant birds became tiny shadows as they hurried home, and here and there the frogs sang themselves to sleep.

It appeared that the wheat fields had been mostly harvested, so the festival would undoubtedly begin soon — perhaps even as soon as the day after tomorrow.

Before Lawrence lay the expanses of the village of Pasloe's fertile wheat fields. The more abundant the harvest, the more prosperous the villagers. Furthermore, the noble who managed the land, one Count Ehrendott, was a famous area eccentric who enjoyed working in the fields himself. Naturally the festival also enjoyed his support, and every year it was a riot of wine and song.

Lawrence had not once participated in it, though. Unfortunately, outsiders were not permitted.

"Ho there, good work!" Lawrence called out to a farmer driving a cart heaped high with wheat in the corner of one of the fields. It was well-ripened wheat. Those who had invested in wheat futures could breath a sigh of relief.

"What's that?"

"Might you tell me where to find Yarei?" Lawrence asked.

"Oh, Yarei'll be over yonder — see where the crowd is gathering? That field. It's all youngsters at his place this year. Whoever's slowest will wind up being the Holo!" said the farmer good-naturedly, his tan face smiling. It was the kind of guileless smile a merchant could never manage.

Lawrence thanked the farmer with his best trader's smile, and turned his horse toward Yarei's place.

Just as the farmer had said, there was a crowd gathering within its confines, and they were shouting something. They seemed to be making sport of the few who were still working the field, but it wasn't ridicule at their lateness. The jeering was part of the festival.

As Lawrence lazily approached the crowd, he was able to make out their shouting.

"There's a wolf! A wolf!"

"A wolf lies there!"

"Who will be the last and catch the wolf? Who, who, who?" the villagers shouted, their faces so cheerful one wondered if they were drunk. None of them noticed Lawrence pulling his cart up behind the crowd.

What they so enthusiastically called a wolf was in fact not a wolf at all. Had it been real, no one would have been laughing.

The wolf was the harvest god, and according to village legend, it resided within the last stalk of wheat to be reaped. Whoever cut that stalk down would be possessed by the wolf, it was said.

"It's the last bundle!"

"Mind you, don't cut too far!"

"Holo flees from the greedy hand!"

"Who, who, who will catch the wolf?"

"It's Yarei! Yarei, Yarei, Yarei!"

Lawrence got off his wagon and peered at the crowd just as Yarei caught the last bundle of wheat. His face was black with sweat and soil as he grinned and hefted the wheat high, threw his head back, and howled.

"Awooooooo!"

"It's Holo! Holo, Holo, Holo!"

"Awooooooo!"

"Holo the wolf is here! Holo the wolf is here!"

"Catch it, now! Catch it quick!"

"Don't let it escape!"

The shouting men suddenly gave chase after Yarei.

The god of the bountiful harvest, once cornered, would possess a human and try to escape. Capture it and it would remain for another year.

None knew if this god truly existed. But this was an old tradition in the area.

Lawrence had traveled far and wide, so he put no stock in the teachings of the Church, but his faith in superstition was greater even than that of the farmers here. Too many times had he crossed mountains only to arrive in towns and find the price of his goods dropping precipitously. It was enough to make anyone superstitious.

Thus he didn't bat an eye at traditions that true believers or Church officials would've found outrageous.

But it was inconvenient that Yarei was this year's Holo. Now Yarei would be locked in a granary stocked with treats until the festival was over — close to a week — and would be impossible to talk to.

15

I WAS TRADING SALT THERE.

A HALF-DAY'S TRAVEL EAST OF HERE, THERE'S A SMALL VILLAGE IN THE MOUNTAINS.

THESE ARE THE PELTS I RECEIVED IN EXCHANGE.

THE LEFT-OVER SALT?

AND THIS?

MM.

16

AH, THIS IS THE COLD-RESISTANT WHEAT I RECEIVED FROM THE VILLAGE.

...SO I RECKON THERE'S DEMAND FOR IT.

CROPS IN THE NORTHWEST COUNTRY SUSTAINED HEAVY FROST DAMAGE LAST YEAR...

HM. VERY WELL.

YOU MAY PASS.

GOKUN (GULP)

WHAT WAS THAT?

NORMALLY, AN HONORABLE KNIGHT WOULDN'T BE ALL THE WAY OUT HERE.

SO, HAS SOMETHING HAPPENED TO OCCASION YOUR POST?

!

I SHOULD THANK YOU.

MMM. DELI-CIOUS.

GOT HIM.

THUS I'VE BEEN ENTRUSTED WITH THE GUARD.

THERE'S TELL OF A BIG PAGAN FESTIVAL APPROACHING.

SADLY, I KNOW NOTHING.

DO YOU KNOW ANYTHING OF THIS FESTIVAL?

PAGANS ARE A COWARDLY LOT, AFTER ALL.

PERHAPS IT TRULY IS BEING HELD IN SECRET, THEN.

STILL, A PAGAN FESTIVAL, THEY SAY...?

BUSINESS EVERYWHERE WILL SUFFER.

WHAT'S THAT?

HO THERE, GOOD WORK!

MIGHT YOU TELL ME WHERE TO FIND YAREI?

OH, YAREI'LL BE OVER YONDER... SEE WHERE THE CROWD IS GATHERING? THAT FIELD.

LOOKS LIKE THEY'RE HAVIN' A MIGHTY ROUGH TIME OF IT!

IT'S ALL YOUNGSTERS AT HIS PLACE THIS YEAR.

SOMEONE IN THAT FIELD'S GONNA WIND UP BEING THIS YEAR'S "HOLO"!

MY THANKS!

WELCOME TO IT!

THERE IT IS, THE WOLF!

THE WOLF!

......!

THERE'S THE WOLF!

IT'S HOLO!

THE SO-CALLED "PAGAN FESTIVAL" OF PASLOE... WAS A MERE HARVEST CELEBRATION.

CATCH IT QUICK!

HOLO THE WOLF IS HERE!

DON'T LET IT ESCAPE, NOW!

HOLO!

HOLO!!

HOLO!!

ウォォォォォ......'

—AWOOOOOO!

THUS, THE VILLAGER WHO TOOK THE ROLE OF HOLO WAS LOCKED IN A GRANARY STOCKED WITH TREATS FOR A FULL WEEK.

NO-THING FOR IT, I SUP-POSE...

GET IT!!

GOOO!!

CAPTURE THE GOD OF THE HARVEST, AND IT WOULD GUARANTEE NEXT YEAR'S BOUNTY.

HOLO!!

FUUUU (SIIIGH)

GOT IIIIIIT!

SO THE MONASTERY IN THE EAST HAS POSTED A KNIGHT, HAS IT?

ALL FOR A SILLY RUMOR ABOUT A TINY VILLAGE LIKE THIS ONE.

HA HA HA....

HAD I ASSETS ENOUGH, I'D HAVE DONE WELL TO BUY SOME FUTURES HERE.

STILL, IT LOOKS LIKE YOU REAPED QUITE A HARVEST THIS YEAR.

I THOUGHT IT WOULD BE BEST TO LET THE VILLAGE HEAD KNOW.

HE STILL TALKS ABOUT YOU, SOMETIMES— HOW HE OWES YOU FOR THE FAVOR YOU DID US, BACK WHEN WE HAD THE OLD LANDLORD.

YAREI'S ALWAYS THE FIRST TO GIVE YOU THE CREDIT FOR THAT.

UFU FU... AH HA HA....

I'M SORRY, LAWRENCE. YAREI WANTED TO SEE YOU TOO, I RECKON.

I CAN'T CONVINCE YOU TO STAY THE NIGHT?

GIVE HIM MY REGARDS WHEN THE FESTIVAL'S OVER.

IT WOULD'VE BEEN NICE TO DRINK WITH HIM.

GATO (CLUNK)

WE MERCHANTS CAN'T AFFORD NOT TO BE DEVOUT.

IT'S CUSTOM TO CHASE OFF OUTSIDERS ONCE THE FESTIVAL STARTS, NAY?

AT LEAST TAKE THESE, THEN.

SFX: GEFU (BURP)

DON
TEN (TING)
DON (BOOM)
TEN
TEN

GOTO (CLOP)
GOTO
GOTO
GOTO

THE MOON'S GOTTEN HIGH...

BURURU
(NEIGH)

THE ROAD WOULD BE LIVELIER IF YOU COULD TALK, BOY.

MASTER, MAAAS-TER!

OTHERWISE, I'M GONNA START CHARGIN' YOU!

MASTER, I'M PLUM KNACK-ERED!

CAN'T YOU LET ME HAVE A BREAK?

YEAH.

NOW THAT I THINK ABOUT IT, MAYBE SILENCE IS GOLDEN, AFTER ALL...

BUN
(SHAKE)

BUN

GARI
(CRUNCH)

GARI

WHOA!!

WHOA!!

ZAPA
(SLISH)

TSUU
(ZZZ)

BASHA
(SLURP)

BASHA

SEVEN YEARS I'VE BEEN CAMPING WITH YOU...

WITH MY MODEST ABILITY AND THE VAST UNEXPLORED MARKETS, I FEEL MY GREATEST CHALLENGES STILL LIE BEFORE ME.

I TURN TWENTY-FIVE THIS YEAR.

AT TWELVE, I APPRENTICED UNDER A RELATIVE, AND AT EIGHTEEN, I SET OUT ON MY OWN.

THE PEOPLE I'VE MET...THE MERCHANTS I'M INDEBTED TO... THE GIRLS I'VE FALLEN FOR...

YET MY THOUGHTS OFTEN DRIFT TO THE UNIMAGINABLE THINGS THAT HAVE HAPPENED SINCE I FIRST STARTED OUT, SO FULL OF PASSION.

I'D BEST SLEEP.

LATELY, MY SIGHS HAVE GOTTEN MORE FREQUENT.

THAT'S RIGHT, I'VE GOT THESE FURS...MAY AS WELL USE THEM.

SPECIAL THANKS: IMU SANJOU-SAMA

ZU (DRAG)

ZU

ZU

......

SUU
(ZZZ)
スウ...

SUU
スウ...

HEY, YOU THERE! WAKE UP! WHAT ARE YOU PLAYING AT, SLEEPING IN SOMEONE'S CART!?

HRM...

ゆらっ
YURA
(RISE)

OF COURSE...! SHE'S A PROSTITUTE! I'D BEST NOT TOUCH HER.

SH-SHE'S TOO PRETTY TO BE A RUN-AWAY...

ゴク...
GOKU
(GULP)

...WHOA...!

SPICE & WOLF

HAVE YOU NO WINE?

HMPH... 'TIS A GOOD MOON.

FOOD,
THEN
...?
OH
HO...

WERE
YOU TO
BE SOLD
IN TOWN?
DID YOU
ESCAPE?

WHY
DO YOU
SLEEP
IN MY
CART?

I
HAVE
NONE.
AND
WHAT
ARE
YOU?

DRIED
MEAT
...

WHAT,
SO YOU
HAVE
NO WINE
?

GAFU
(CHOMP)

FANGS
!?

HYOI
(SNATCH)

KYORO

KYORO!
(GLANCE)

HA
(GASP)

ME, A DEMON NOW?

AH HA HA HA HA HA!

ARE YOU SOME KIND OF DEMON?

H-HOW IS THAT SO AMUS-ING?

NIKO (SMILE)

MM. AH, I SEE. MY ESCAPE WAS SUC-CESSFUL.

WHAT ARE YOU, I SAY ?

MY APOLO-GIES! I HAD FORGOT-TEN.

I AM CALLED HOLO.

IT HAS BEEN SOME TIME SINCE I'VE TAKEN THIS FORM, BUT, WELL, IT IS QUITE NICE.

HOLO? ...SO SHE'S FROM PASLOE, THEN...... A RUNAWAY, MAYBE?

ARE YOU A GOD?

THAT IS THE NAME OF THIS AREA'S HARVEST GOD.

BUT I AM NOTHING SO GREAT AS A DEITY.

I HAVE LONG BEEN BOUND TO THIS PLACE AND CALLED ITS GOD.

I AM MERELY HOLO.

BUT WITH THOSE EARS AND TAIL, SHE CAN'T HAVE BEEN RAISED AS A HUMAN...

A BOLD GIRL, INDEED. SHE REALLY THINKS SHE'S HOLO.

BURURU (WHINNY)

BY "LONG," DO YOU MEAN THAT YOU WERE BORN HERE?

PERHAPS SHE WAS HIDDEN, RAISED IN SECRET BY HER FAMILY.

IT WAS DESTROYED CENTURIES AGO... THERE'S NO WAY A GIRL FROM THIS TOWN WOULD KNOW OF IT.

I KNEW OF IT FROM AN OLD STORY I'D HEARD AT AN INN IN THE NORTH.

DID SHE SAY "YOI-TSU"!?

DO YOU REMEMBER ANY OTHER PLACES?

AH!

NYOH-HIRA, THERE WAS A TOWN CALLED NYOH-HIRA.

IT WAS A STRANGE TOWN, WITH HOT SPRINGS.

MMM...

IT'S BEEN SO MANY CENTURIES...

I WOULD OFTEN GO TO BATHE IN THEM.

THE HOT SPRINGS OF THE NORTH COUNTRY...

BACHA! (SPLISH!)

PEKI (SNEEZE)

IT IS OF THE WHITE TIP OF MY TAIL THAT I AM PROUDEST. ALL WHO SEE IT, PRAISE IT.

MY EARS ANTICIPATE EVERY MISFORTUNE AND HEAR EVERY LIE, AND I HAVE SAVED MANY FRIENDS FROM MANY DANGERS.

MM. I DO NOT MIND TAKING HUMAN FORM, BUT IT IS UN-AVOID-ABLY COLD.

NOT ENOUGH FUR.

GOSO (SQUIRM)

YOU SAID SOMETHING ABOUT CHANGING FORMS EARLIER— WHAT WAS THAT ABOUT?

HEH HEH...

ASIDE FROM A FEW EXTRA DETAILS, YOU'RE HUMAN.

WHEN ONE SPEAKS OF THE WISEWOLF OF YOITSU, THEY SPEAK OF NONE OTHER THAN ME!

YES?

HOLO, WAS IT?

WHA...?

YOU'RE TELLING ME TO SHOW YOU MY WOLF FORM, ARE YOU NOT?

NO.

ALL YOU HAVE ARE A WOLF'S EARS AND TAIL. IF YOU ARE TRULY A TRANSFORMED WOLF...

IF YOU WERE A PERSON, I WOULD CONSIDER TURNING YOU IN TO THE CHURCH... DEMONS CAUSE CALAMITY, AFTER ALL.

BUT IF YOU ARE REALLY HOLO, GOD OF THE HARVEST, IN HUMAN FORM...

...THEN I NEEDN'T TURN YOU IN.

KOHON (COUGH)

WHAT KIND OF TOKEN?

I REQUIRE FOOD. ONLY A BIT OF WHEAT.

NO ANIMAL CAN CHANGE ITS FORM WITHOUT A TOKEN.

IF YOU ARE TELLING THE TRUTH, YOU SHOULD BE ABLE TO DO SO AS WELL, YES?

FROM WHAT I HAVE HEARD, TRANS-FORMED ANIMALS CAN CHANGE TO THEIR ORIGINAL FORMS.

FRESH ... BLOOD ?

THAT, OR FRESH BLOOD.

OF COURSE NOT!

KUH FU FU...

WHAT, ARE YOU AFRAID?

ヒヒ
ヒヒーン

HIHII
(NEIGH)

HIIN
(NEIGH)

HAA
(PANT)

HAA

HAA

MM...
WHEW...
IT REALLY
DOESN'T
LOOK VERY
GOOD.

WELL?
DO YOU
BELIEVE
ME NOW?

BASHA

BASHA
(SPLASH)

バシャ

AREN'T
YOU THE
DOUBTFUL
ONE. IF YOU
STILL THINK
IT'S AN
ILLUSION,
GO AHEAD
AND TOUCH
IT.

UH...
MM...

BARI

BARI (CRUNCH)

ARE YOU ...

...REALLY A GOD...?

ZU (SHFF)

ZU ZU ZU ZU

I'M NO GOD.

BUT...THE REAL HOLO SHOULD BE IN YAREI NOW.

I AM MERELY BIGGER THAN MY COMRADES— BIGGER AND CLEVERER.

HEH HEH HEH. I AM HOLO THE WISE-WOLF!

THE WOLF RESIDES IN THE ONE WHO CUTS THE LAST WHEAT STALK, THEY SAY...

I KNOW WELL MY OWN LIMITATIONS.

SO, WHAT THINK YOU?

NOT WHILE ANY WERE WATCHING.

USUALLY I CANNOT ESCAPE FROM THERE.

AND IT IS ALSO TRUE THAT DURING THIS HARVEST I WAS WITHIN THE LAST WHEAT TO BE HARVESTED.

IT IS TRUE THAT I LIVE WITHIN THE WHEAT. WITHOUT IT, I CANNOT LIVE.

HOWEVER, THERE IS AN EXCEPTION.

THAT'S WHY THEY SAY IT, YOU KNOW, THE VILLAGERS. "IF YOU CUT TOO GREEDILY, YOU WON'T CATCH THE HARVEST GOD, AND IT WILL ESCAPE."

IF THERE IS NEARBY A LARGER SHEAF OF WHEAT THAN THE LAST ONE TO BE HARVESTED, I CAN MOVE UNSEEN TO THAT WHEAT.

IF YOU HADN'T BEEN THERE, I WOULD NEVER HAVE ESCAPED.

!

SO THAT IS HOW IT WAS DONE. I SUPPOSE ONE COULD CALL YOU MY "SAVIOR."

UH...
UM...

BA
(FWIP)

.....YES?

I MUST
ASK
YOU ONE
THING.

TON
(THUD)

GATA
(CLATTER)

WELL?

IF YOU
LEAVE THE
VILLAGE,
WILL THEY
STILL BE
ABLE TO
RAISE
WHEAT?

THE VILLAGE'S ABUNDANT HARVESTS WILL CONTINUE WITHOUT ME.

ER... WHAT'S WRONG?

GYU CLENCH

.......IS THAT SO?

EVENTUALLY I WISHED TO LEAVE, BUT FOR THE SAKE OF THE VILLAGE'S WHEAT I STAYED.

LONG DID I STAY IN THAT VILLAGE; AS MANY YEARS AS I HAVE HAIRS ON MY TAIL.

LONG AGO, YOU SEE, I MADE A PROMISE WITH A YOUTH OF THE VILLAGE, THAT I WOULD ENSURE THE VILLAGE'S HARVEST.

AND SO I KEPT MY PROMISE!

I...I AM THE WOLF THAT LIVES IN THE WHEAT. MY KNOWLEDGE OF WHEAT, OF THINGS THAT GROW IN THE GROUND, IS SECOND TO NONE.

THAT IS WHY I MADE THE VILLAGE'S FIELDS SO MAGNIFICENT, AS I PROMISED.

BUT WHENEVER THE HARVEST WAS POOR, THE VILLAGERS ATTRIBUTED IT TO MY CAPRICES...

FORCING THE LAND TO PRODUCE REQUIRES COMPENSATION.

BUT TO DO THAT, OCCASIONALLY THE HARVEST MUST BE POOR.

I CAN STAND IT NO LONGER. I LONG AGO FULFILLED MY PROMISE!

...AND IT HAS ONLY GOTTEN WORSE IN RECENT YEARS. I HAVE BEEN WANTING TO LEAVE!

SOME YEARS AGO... THAT WOULD COINCIDE WITH COUNT EHRENDOTT INTRODUCING NEW FARMING TECHNIQUES...

THE VILLAGE'S GOOD HARVESTS WILL CONTINUE.

...BUT THAT WILL BE THEIR OWN DOING.

THERE WILL BE A POOR YIELD EVERY FEW YEARS...

BOFU (WHUMP)

THE LAND DOESN'T NEED ME!

AND THEY'LL OVERCOME IT ON THEIR OWN!

AND THE PEOPLE CERTAINLY DON'T NEED ME EITHER!!

SORRY.

IN ANY CASE, SETTING ASIDE THE QUESTION OF WHETHER OR NOT THAT'S ALL TRUE...

KI (GLARE)

I WISH TO RETURN NORTH.

I UNDER-STAND YOUR RESENT-MENT.

BUT WHERE DO YOU PLAN TO GO, HAVING LEFT THE VILLAGE?

PIKU! (PERK)

I WISH TO RETURN HOME.

TO MY BIRTH-PLACE. THE FOREST OF YOI-TSU.

SO MANY YEARS HAVE PASSED THAT I CAN NO LONGER COUNT THEM...

BUT I'D LIKE TO TRAVEL A BIT. I'VE COME ALL THE WAY TO THIS DISTANT PLACE, AFTER ALL.

AND SURELY MUCH HAS CHANGED OVER THE MONTHS AND YEARS, SO IT WOULD BE GOOD TO BROADEN MY PERSPECTIVE.

...I'D LIKE TO TRAVEL WITH YOU.

SO LONG AS YOU'LL NOT TAKE ME BACK TO PASLOE OR TURN ME IN TO THE CHURCH...

YOU'RE A WANDERING MERCHANT, ARE YOU NOT?

I CANNOT MAKE THIS DECISION QUICKLY.

IT IS GOOD TO BE CAUTIOUS.

...OR, IN MY CASE, A WOLF.

I DON'T BELIEVE YOU'RE SO COLD AS TO TURN A PERSON IN NEED AWAY.

BUT I NEVER MIS-READ A PER-SON.

I HAVE TO SLEEP IN THERE, TOO, SO MOVE OVER.

SURELY YOU'LL NOT TELL ME TO SLEEP OUTSIDE.

PIKO (POP)

BURURU (NEEEIGH)

I DON'T KNOW HOW MUCH OF IT IS AN ACT... BUT IT'S NOT ALL LIES, ANYWAY.

SO LONG AS I DON'T AWAKEN TO FIND ALL MY GOODS GONE...

OH,
YOU ARE
AWAKE.

DID
SHE
......!?

BUN
(SHAKE)

BUN

THESE TROUSERS, THOUGH— THEY GET IN THE WAY OF MY TAIL. MIGHT I PUT A HOLE IN THEM?

!?

...FINEST CLOTHES...

...ARE MY...

THOSE...

YOU'RE A MERCHANT THROUGH AND THROUGH, THAT'S SURE ENOUGH. I KNOW JUST WHAT YOU ANTICIPATE WITH THAT EXPRESSION ON YOUR FACE.

HRM. WELL, FORTUNATELY THEY'RE STILL LARGE. I'LL FIND A WAY TO MAKE THEM WORK.

SO, I WISH TO TRAVEL WITH YOU.

MAY I?

YOU'LL HAVE TO EARN YOUR KEEP, THOUGH.

THIS MUST BE SOME KIND OF FATE. VERY WELL.

I EXPECT THE GOD OF ABUNDANT HARVESTS TO BRING AN ABUNDANT HARVEST TO MY COIN PURSE.

THE LIFE OF A MERCHANT ISN'T EASY.

BUFUU (SNORT)

BURURU (NEEEIGH)

I'M NOT SO SHAMELESS AS TO THOUGHT- LESSLY FREELOAD.

BUWA (FWUMP)

GOTO (CCLUNK)

PFFT!

AH-HA- HA-HA- HA-HA!

DIDN'T REALLY NOTICE BEFORE, BUT SHE'S RATHER SMALL.

...AND I HAVE MY PRIDE.

CHIMA (TINY)

I'M HOLO THE WISE- WOLF...

MM. LAWRENCE. I SHALL SING YOUR PRAISES FOR ALL ETERNITY.

LAWRENCE. KRAFT LAWRENCE.

WHEN I'M WORKING, I GO BY LAWRENCE.

...MADE A BIT OF A SPECTACLE OF HERSELF YESTERDAY.

THOUGH THIS PROUD WOLF...

IN ANY CASE, IT IS GOOD TO MEET YOU...

...ER...

SHE SEEMED ODDLY SERIOUS.

IT WAS DIFFICULT TO TELL IF SHE WAS BEING CHILDISH OR CUNNING.

HER GIRLISH HAND IS SMALL AND WARM.

OH!

GOTO (CLOP)

GOTO

THE RIVER IS IN A FOUL TEMPER. 'TWOULD BE BEST TO CROSS A SHORT DISTANCE FROM HERE.

HIHHHHIN (NEEEIGH)

WHA...? YOU SHOULD HAVE SAID SO SOONER!

AT ANY RATE, IT WILL SOON RAIN.

WE SHOULD MAKE HASTE.

SFX: BASHI (SNAP)

THE DRIVER'S SEAT IS TOO BIG FOR ONE PERSON, BUT SLIGHTLY TOO SMALL FOR TWO.

I ONLY JUST NOTICED THAT.

THE RAIN
CLOUDS ARE
FOLLOWING
US...

JUST
A LITTLE
MORE, AND
WE'D REACH
MY FRIEND'S
LODGING
HOUSE,
BUT...

GUI
(YANK)

GUESS IT
CAN'T BE
HELPED.

!

...DON'T
SPEAK
ANY MORE
THAN YOU
HAVE TO.

IF WE'RE
CAUGHT,
THEY WON'T
LET ME
OFF EASILY,
EITHER.

ZAAAA
...

HEH!
THIS SHALL
PROVE TO
BE MOST
INTEREST-
ING.

THANK YOU SO MUCH.

PLEASE EXCUSE MY WIFE'S RUDENESS. SHE IS ASHAMED TO SHOW THE BURNS ON HER FACE.

I SEE... YOU HAVE MY SYMPATHIES. WE HAVE ONE ROOM THAT IS SOMEWHAT REMOVED FROM THE OTHERS.

YOU MAY USE IT, IF YOU WISH.

GORO (ROLL)

ゴ゛ロ゛

GORO

ゴ゛ロ゛

THANKS BE TO GOD.

IT'S ME. I'M COMING IN.

ココン

MM.

BA
(WHAP)

...AND MARTENS LIVE IN THE MOUNTAINS, MOUNTAINS WHERE MY KIND LIVE AS WELL.

THEY WERE GOOD MARTEN SKINS...

JAAA

WELL, THAT'S TRUE.

WILL THEY SELL HIGH?

OH, THAT'S RIGHT. WHAT SHALL WE DO WITH THAT WHEAT SHEAF?

ZU
(SLIP)

CHIRA
(GLANCE)

JAAA
(SPLOOSH)

I HARDLY KNOW. I'M NO FUR MERCHANT, AM I?

BUT SHOULD IT BE EATEN OR BURNED, I WILL LIKELY DISAPPEAR.

AS LONG AS I LIVE, THE WHEAT WILL NEITHER ROT NOR WITHER.

I'LL THRESH IT AND PUT THE GRAINS IN A POUCH, THEN.

I SEE.

IF IT'S IN THE WAY, YOU COULD THRESH IT AND KEEP IT SAFE SOMEWHERE; THAT MIGHT BE BETTER.

'TWOULD BE A BOON. STILL BETTER TO HANG IT 'ROUND MY NECK.

YOU SHOULD HOLD IT, RIGHT?

COULD WE SET ASIDE A BIT FOR SALE?

『GUI (GRAB)』

I'D HOPED TO SELL SOME OF IT ELSEWHERE, THOUGH.

CROPS ARE FOUND IN A REGION PRECISELY BECAUSE THEY GROW WELL THERE.

THEY'LL SOON WITHER. NO USE TAKING THEM ELSE-WHERE.

ばさっ
BASA (FWAP)

ばさっ
BASA

！

WITH THIS RAIN, THERE SHOULD BE A FIRE GOING IN THE FURNACE.

LET'S GO DRY OURSELVES IN THE GREAT ROOM.

べち。
BECHO

べちょ
BECHO (STICK)

GUI GYANK!

HUP!

MM, A GOOD IDEA, THAT.

WHAT'S SO FUNNY?

FUH FU FU

OH? WHAT WOULD YOU HAVE DONE?

...COVER UP MY FACE BECAUSE OF BURNS.

HEH, I WOULD NEVER HAVE THOUGHT TO...

...JUST LIKE MY EARS OR TAIL. PROOF OF MY UNIQUE-NESS.

THE BURNS WOULD BECOME PART OF ME...

I KNOW WHAT YOU ARE THINKING.

DOKI (WHUMP)
HMMM...

WANT TO INJURE ME AND SEE FOR YOURSELF?

I'M A MAN. I COULD NEVER INJURE SUCH A BEAUTIFUL FACE.

FUWA
(WAFT)

TOSU
(BUMP)

WHY, YOU—

HYOI
(DODGE)

YOU MAY HAVE BEEN CAUGHT IN THE RAIN, BUT YOU STILL SMELL FOUL. A WOLF CAN TELL THESE THINGS.

?

KUN
KUN
(SNIFF)

KUN

KUN

THE BEARD, THOUGH, IS QUITE NICE.

EVEN A WOLF KNOWS TO KEEP ITS COAT CLEAN. YOU'RE A GOOD MAN, AYE...

KURU
(FWIP)

...BUT YOU NEED TO KEEP NEAT.

I DARESAY I'D PREFER IT A BIT LONGER, THOUGH.

HEE HEE HEE!

HER HEH!

P! (POINK)

...LIKE SO, LIKE A WOLF.

GA
THUNK

I AM
HOLO THE
WISEWOLF!

THERE WILL
BE MANY
PEOPLE
AROUND THE
FURNACE.
BEST NOT
TO LET
ANYTHING
SLIP.

LONG AGO
I TRAVELED
CLEAR TO
PASLOE IN
HUMAN FORM.
WORRY NOT!

TON
(THMP)

AHA!

...AND GOT MARTEN FURS IN TRADE.

YES, I DELIVERED SALT FROM THERE TO MY CUSTOMER...

SO YOU'RE HERE FROM YORENZ, THEN?

OH HO, INTEREST-ING!

THAT DEPENDS ON HOW CANNY THE MERCHANT.

STILL, GOING ALL THE WAY BACK TO YORENZ, ISN'T THAT RATHER ARDUOUS?

RATHER, I'D ALREADY SOLD A MEASURE OF WHEAT TO A DIFFERENT BRANCH OF THE SAME COMPANY IN ANOTHER CITY— BUT WHEN I SOLD THE WHEAT, I TOOK NO PAYMENT; NEITHER DID I PAY FOR THE SALT.

WHEN I BOUGHT THE SALT IN YORENZ, I PAID NO MONEY.

SO I COMPLETED TWO SEPARATE DEALS WITH NO MONEY EXCHANGED.

PASLOE

YORENZ

THE TRANSFER OF MONEY BETWEEN BRANCHES OF THE COMPANY IS HANDLED INTERNALLY.

...HAS NEVER EMPLOYED SUCH A STRANGE METHOD.

I LIVE IN THE CITY OF PERENZZO, AND MY VINEYARD...

WHAT A STRANGE CONTRIVANCE...

I SEE...

AS THE OWNER OF A VINEYARD, YOU'D NEED TO BE CAREFUL NOT TO LET VINTNERS CLAIM YOUR GRAPES TO BE POOR AND BUY THEM CHEAPLY.

THIS BARTER SYSTEM WAS INVENTED BY MERCHANTS WHO NEEDED A CONVENIENT WAY TO DEAL WITH PEOPLE FROM MANY DIFFERENT LANDS.

WILL WE BE ALL RIGHT?

WE HAVE SUCH ARGUMENTS EVERY YEAR.

YES.

NEXT TIME YOU'RE IN PERENZZO, DO COME BY FOR A VISIT.

LAWRENCE, WAS IT?

WE'D WELCOME YOU MOST HAPPILY.

IT'S QUITE A PROBLEM, HA-HA-HA!

I'D LOVE TO HEAR MORE OF YOUR TRAVELS...

...HIS MIGHT BE A GRAND HOUSE INDEED.

MOST NOBLES DON'T INTRODUCE THEM-SELVES, BUT...

I SHALL, THANK YOU.

MY WIFE APPEARS TIRED......

EXCUSE US.

SFX: GASHI (GRAB)

ゴト (CLINK)

バタン (SHUT)

ONCE OUR CLOTHES ARE A BIT DRIER, SHALL WE TAKE DINNER IN OUR ROOM?

WE CAN BORROW A STOVE AND COOK SOMETHING!

NIKA (GRIN)

HEH-HEH, YOU'RE NOT A MAN TO BE TRIFLED WITH, MASTER!

PIKU
(PERK)

FAR FROM IT, MASTER!

I'M MERELY A TRAVELING MERCHANT LIKE ANY OTHER.

THINKING THAT IT'S TRADERS LIKE YOU THAT I'LL BE GOING UP AGAINST IN THE FUTURE, WHY, IT'S HARD NOT TO DESPAIR!

YET YOU SLIPPED RIGHT IN.

I'D BEEN WANTING TO SPEAK WITH HIM FOR SOME TIME BUT COULDN'T FIND THE OPPORTUNITY.

YOU JUST HAVE TO KEEP AT IT.

DID HE PULL THAT TOOTH ON PURPOSE?

BUT I'M STILL EATING, SOME-HOW.

THAT'S NOTHING— WHEN I WAS STARTING OUT, ALL THE ESTABLISHED MERCHANTS SEEMED LIKE MONSTERS TO ME. HALF OF THEM STILL DO.

I'M LAWRENCE.

AND YOU'VE PROBABLY FIGURED IT OUT, BUT I'M JUST STARTING OUT AS A MERCHANT. BEGGING YOUR IN-DULGENCE, SIR!

OH, BY THE WAY, I'M ZHEREN.

HEH HEH, IT'S A RELIEF TO HEAR YOU SAY SO, SIR.

MY, A WIFE AND A MERCHANT BOTH?

MY WIFE...

...HOLO.

...THEN IS THIS YOUR COMPANION?

S...

SO...

THIS GUY...!

ZUI (ZIP)

SURELY YOU CAN LET ME HAVE A LOOK AT HER.

HEH-HEH, BUT IT IS A MAN'S INSTINCT TO WANT TO SEE HIDDEN THINGS. GOD HAS LED US TOGETHER HERE, AFTER ALL.

STILL, COVERING YOUR WIFE IN A CLOAK THIS WAY, SHE MUST BE VERY PRECIOUS TO YOU.

SHE IS AN ECCENTRIC AND PREFERS THE WAGON TO THE VILLAGE HOME.

...AND THUS 'TIS SOMETHING I CANNOT DO.

TO SHOW MY FACE IN PUBLIC WOULD DASH MANY DREAMS...

...IS HAPPIEST BEFORE THE JOURNEY; THE DOG'S BARK FIERCER THAN THE DOG ITSELF, AND A WOMAN MOST BEAUTIFUL FROM BEHIND.

キョトン
~ KYOTON
(STUNNED)

KU FU FU!

IT'S ALL I CAN DO TO AVOID BEING QUITE HENPECKED.

HEH-HEH... YOUR WIFE IS SOMETHING ELSE, MASTER.

CAN YOU SPARE A MOMENT TO HEAR MY TALE?

YES, WELL ...

IT'S CERTAINLY PROVIDENTIAL THAT I'VE MET THE BOTH OF YOU.

SPICE & WOLF

I'M COMING IN.

cr creak

95

AGU
(CHEW)

あぐ

あぐ

くん
KUN
(SNIFF)

HM? SOMETHING SMELLS GOOD.

IT IS NOT AS THOUGH WE WOLVES EAT MEAT YEAR-ROUND.

AYE.

SO WOLVES FIND BAKED BREAD DELICIOUS, DO THEY?

あぐっ
AFU
(CHOMP)

はぐっ
HAFU
(GOBBLE)

AND THE CROPS THAT HUMANS RAISE ARE BETTER STILL THAN TREE BUDS.

WE EAT TENDER BUDS FROM TREES. WE EAT FISH.

んぐっ
NGU
(CHOKE)

はっ
HAAAAH (PANT)

はっ
HAAAAH

ARE YOU ALL RIGHT!?

GUH!

バタ
(BATA (WHAP))

バタ
BATA

バタ
BATA

HERE.

ビリ
(TWITCH)
ビリ
BIRI
BIRI

WOLVES SWALLOW THINGS WHOLE, AFTER ALL.

MM, WELL...

HA HA HA

WHEW. RATHER SURPRISING, THAT. HUMAN THROATS ARE SO NARROW. IT'S QUITE INCONVENIENT.

ILL-FATED, EH?

BUT I'VE CHOKED ON BREAD IN THE PAST. IT'S TRUE. I SUPPOSE RYE BREAD AND I ARE ILL-FATED.

...EE LACK DEEZE, SHO WE CANNUT SHEW AT OUR LEAZURE.

ニッ
NIU (STRETCH)

OH, RIGHT. ON THE WAY TO THE STOVE...

ゴソ (GOSO)
ゴソ (GOSO)
ゴソ GOSO (RUMMAGE)
ゴツ
ゴツ
ゴツ

SFX: NYU (REACH)

OH. THE WHEAT.

WHA?

TOSA (TOSS)
トサッ

!

MUSHA
むしゃ

MM, MY THANKS.

BUT THIS TAKES PRECEDENCE.

MUSHA
むしゃ
MUSHA (MUNCH)

AND HERE'S A STRAP, SO YOU CAN WORK OUT A WAY TO HANG IT AROUND YOUR NECK.

ALL THAT RIGHT THERE COST PLENTY.

YOUR FUR IS QUITE NICE...IT'S FLUFFED OUT NOW THAT IT'S DRY.

ぱさ
(PATA (WHAP))

ぱさ
(PATA)

ぱさ
(PATA)

......

WELL, IT'S A CREDIT TO YOUR EYE FOR QUALITY THAT YOU CAN TELL AS MUCH, THEN!

SO, WHAT IS IT YOU WANT TO ASK ME?

AHEM!

HM? OH, MORE OR LESS.

SO IS IT TRUE THAT YOU CAN TELL TRUTH FROM LIES?

SO, HOW GOOD AT IT ARE YOU?

WELL, I KNOW THAT WHAT YOU SAID ABOUT MY TAIL JUST NOW WAS NOT MEANT AS PRAISE.

IT'S NOT PERFECT, THOUGH.

YOU MAY BELIEVE ME OR NOT... AS YOU WISH.

SO LET ME ASK YOU THIS— WAS THE LAD'S STORY TRUE?

HEH! HEH!

OH.

THE ONE WHO SPOKE TO US BY THE FURNACE.

"LAD," YOU SAY.

THE LAD?

IS SOMETHING FUNNY?

FROM WHERE I STAND, YOU'RE BOTH BUT LADS.

AS FOR YOUR LAD...

I DARESAY YOU'RE A BIT MORE GROWN THAN HE, THOUGH.

...IT SEEMS TO ME HE IS LYING.

I KNEW IT.

ZHEREN HAD SPOKEN ABOUT AN OPPORTUNITY FOR PROFIT.

HE SAID THERE WAS A CERTAIN SILVER COIN IN CIRCULATION THAT WAS DUE TO BE REPLACED BY A COIN WITH A HIGHER CONCENTRATION OF SILVER.

ISSUER'S GUARANTEED VALUE

NEW   OLD

NEW   OLD

THE ISSUER IS OBLIGED TO EXCHANGE EQUAL AMOUNTS OF THE OLD CURRENCY FOR THE NEW.

IF THE STORY WAS TRUE, THE OLD SILVER COINS WERE OF POORER QUALITY THAN THEIR REPLACE-MENTS, BUT THEIR FACE VALUE WOULD BE THE SAME.

EXCHANGE VALUE AGAINST FOREIGN CURRENCIES
(PROPORTIONAL TO SILVER CONTENT)

HOWEVER, WHEN BEING EXCHANGED FOR OTHER CURRENCIES, THE NEW SILVER COINS WOULD BE WORTH MORE THAN THE OLD.

NEW   OLD

NEW   OLD

SILVER CONTENT DETERMINES VALUE ON THE CURRENCY EXCHANGE MARKET.

EXCHANGE

OLD SILVER CURRENCY

OTHER FOREIGN CURRENCY

NEW   OLD

EXCHANGE OLD CURRENCY FOR NEW FROM ISSUER.

PROFIT   EXCHANGE

OTHER FOREIGN CURRENCY

NEW SILVER CURRENCY

THUS, ONE COULD BUY UP THE OLD CURRENCY IN BULK, THEN EXCHANGE IT FOR THE NEW COINS, THUS PROFITING FROM THE DIFFERENCE IN EXCHANGE VALUE.

I DON'T KNOW WHICH PART IS A LIE, THOUGH, NOR DO I UNDERSTAND THE FINER POINTS OF THE CONVERSATION.

YOU DON'T UNDERSTAND WHY HE'S LYING... NO?

BUT STILL...

GUESS I WASN'T EXPECTING YOU TO...

WELL, CURRENCY SPECULATION ISN'T RARE IN AND OF ITSELF.

WHEN SOMEONE'S LYING, WHAT'S IMPORTANT IS NOT THE CONTENT OF THE LIE, BUT THE REASONING BEHIND IT.

HOW MANY YEARS DO YOU THINK IT TOOK ME TO UNDERSTAND THAT?

HEH-HEHN!

OH? YOU MAY HAVE CALLED THAT ZHEREN PERSON A LAD...

I'M GLAD YOU'RE NOT MY BUSINESS RIVAL.

...BUT YOU'RE BOTH THE SAME TO ME.

IF I WERE NOT HERE, WHAT WOULD YOU DO?

AND WHY IS THAT?

MM...

FIRST I'D WORK OUT WHETHER IT WAS TRUE OR NOT, THEN I'D PRETEND TO BELIEVE HIS STORY.

...BUT I CAN STILL COME OUT AHEAD IF I KEEP MY EYES AND EARS OPEN.

IF IT'S TRUE, I CAN TURN A PROFIT JUST BY GOING ALONG WITH IT. IF IT'S A LIE, THEN SOMEONE SOMEWHERE IS UP TO SOMETHING ...

AH...

MM. AND GIVEN THAT I *AM* HERE, AND I'VE TOLD YOU HE'S LYING, THEN...

SEE, THERE WAS NOTHING OVER WHICH TO AGONIZE SO. EITHER WAY YOU'LL BE PRETENDING TO ACCEPT HIS PROPOSAL.

HEH.

SFX: GA (GOBBLE) GA

POI (TOSS)

I AM HOLO THE WISEWOLF! HOW MANY TIMES LONGER DO YOU THINK I HAVE LIVED THAN YOU?

HYOI (SNATCH)

I'LL BE TAKING THIS LAST PIECE OF BREAD.

FEELS LIKE MY APPRENTICE DAYS ALL OVER AGAIN...

109

GASH!
(BRUSH)
ガシ

ガシ
GASH!

CHIRI
(SCRAPE)
チリ

チー
CHIRI

BASHA

BASHA
(SPLASH)

LORD, GRANT MY HUSBAND COURAGE.

IT'S GOTTEN A BIT MORE IMPORTANT, THE CHURCH HAS.

IT WAS NOT SO WHEN I CAME THROUGH HERE FROM THE NORTH.

NO.

THE CHURCH HAS ALWAYS BEEN IMPORT- ANT.

CHARIN (CLINK)

HAVE YOU YOURSELF CHANGED?

PON (PAT)

I SUPPOSE THIS IS A SIGN OF THE TIMES, THEN... MUCH HAS CHANGED.

THEN I'M SURE YOUR HOMELAND HASN'T CHANGED, EITHER.

'TWOULD BE A DISGRACE TO THE NAME WISEWOLF TO BE COMFORTED BY YOU, THOUGH.

WE'LL SIGN THE FORMAL CONTRACT BEFORE A PUBLIC WITNESS.

THERE'S NO NEED FOR HIM TO SLOW DOWN ON OUR ACCOUNT.

IT RAINED ALL DAY YESTERDAY, SO HE'LL MAKE BETTER TIME ON FOOT THAN WE CAN IN THE WAGON.

ARE WE NOT GOING WITH HIM?

THEY WAKE IN THE DAWN AIR...

...WORK THEIR FIELDS IN THE MORNING AIR, PULL THE WEEDS IN THE AFTERNOON AIR...

...TWIST ROPE IN THE RAINY AIR. THEY WORRY OVER THEIR CROPS IN THE WINDY AIR...

...REJOICE OVER THE BUDDING SHOOTS IN THE SPRING AIR, ENJOY THE LENGTHENING STALKS IN THE SUMMER AIR...

...CELEBRATE THE HARVEST IN THE AUTUMN AIR, AND IN THE WINTER AIR THEY WAIT FOR SPRING.

...LIKE ME.

THEY THINK NOT OF TIME— THEY NOTE ONLY THE AIR...

SFX: GOTO (THUNK) GOTO

GA (THUNK)

GARA (RATTLE)

GA

BECHA

BECHA (SPLISH)

'TIS FINE FUR.

YOU'RE QUICK ENOUGH, BUT YOU LACK EXPERIENCE.

HAAAAH (SIIIGH)

AH-HA-HA-HA-HA! YOU *ARE* RATHER QUICK, AREN'T YOU?

STILL, ONE WILL GROW WISER WITH AGE.

HOW MANY HUNDREDS OF YEARS DO YOU THINK IT WILL TAKE?

JARA
(CLINK)

HAVE THEY NO KING HERE?

ほ〜 OHHHH!

THE ONES WHO RULE HERE ARE NOBLES AND MERCHANTS.

HEH HEH.

IS THIS YOUR FIRST TIME COMING TO A CITY OF THIS SIZE?

GOTO (THUNK) ゴット

ゴット GOTO

HEH. I'LL JUST SAY YOUR INTENTIONS ARE ADMIRABLE.

IF I TELL HER I'VE BEEN TO CITIES MANY TIMES THE SIZE OF THIS ONE, SHE'LL JUST THINK I'M MAKING FUN OF HER.

TIMES SURELY CHANGE. IN MY DAY, A CITY THIS LARGE WOULD HAVE BEEN RULED BY A KING.

GOTO GOTO

GOTO
CHUNG

GATA
(RATTLE)

IS IT ALL PICKED NEARBY?

THERE'S QUITE A COLLECTION OF FRUIT!

SURELY YOU HAVE FRUIT IN THE NORTH, AS WELL.

GATA
GOTO

KUN
(SNIFF)

KUN

THERE IS MUCH FRUIT IN THE SOUTH, AND GOOD.

IT'S BECAUSE PAZZIO IS THE GATEWAY TO THE SOUTH. YOU CAN EVEN SEE FRUIT FROM REGIONS NEARLY IMPOSSIBLE TO VISIT.

WE WOLVES CAN'T DO SUCH WORK, SO WE HAVE TO TAKE IT FROM THE VILLAGES.

AYE, BUT IT'S TOUGH AND BITTER. TO MAKE IT SWEET, IT MUST BE DRIED AND CURED.

ONCE WE FOUND A RED, FANG-SHAPED FRUIT AMONG THE CARGO OF A SHIP-WRECK.

WE ATE IT, AND REGRETTED IT LOUD AND LONG!

I WOULD THINK WOLVES WOULD PREFER SPICY THINGS. IT'S BEARS THAT CRAVE SWEETS.

WE DUNKED OUR HEADS IN THE RIVER AND DECIDED HUMANS WERE TERRIFYING, INDEED.

AH, HOT PEPPERS. EXPENSIVE THOSE.

WE DON'T LIKE SPICY FOOD.

KYU (GRIP)

GOTO GOTO

IF IT'S RED FRUIT WE'RE TALKING ABOUT, I'D RATHER HAVE THOSE.

THEY LOOK RATHER TOOTHSOME, NO?

WASA (SNIFF)

WASA

ARE THEY NOT?

OH, THOSE ARE FINE APPLES.

SPEAKING OF APPLES...

......

UKI (GIDDY)

UKI

GOTO GOTO (THUNK)

I'M NOT SURE WHERE THEY WERE FROM, BUT IF THEY TURNED OUT LIKE THESE, HE'S SURELY DOUBLED HIS MONEY. I SHOULD'VE DONE THE SAME.

?

...I HAD A FRIEND WHO INVESTED MORE THAN HALF HIS WORTH IN APPLES.

GOTO

CHIRA

GOTO

CHIRA (GLANCE)

HMPH...... WELL, THAT'S MOST UNFORTUNATE...

THE AMOUNT OF MONEY THEY RAISE DECIDES THE QUANTITY AND TYPE OF CARGO...

YOU SEE, A GROUP OF MERCHANTS WILL SOMETIMES POOL THEIR MONEY TO HIRE A SHIP.

GOTO

GOTO

SOWA (FIDGET)
SOWA

BUT THE RISK WAS VERY HIGH. IF IT WERE ME, I WOULD'VE TRANSPORTED THEM BY SHIP.

HOW-EVER, THERE IS PROFIT TO BE HAD. I'VE TWICE TRAVELED BY SEA THAT WAY, SO...

...BUT UNLIKE LAND TRANSPORT, IF THERE IS AN ACCIDENT YOU MAY LOSE LIVES AS WELL AS MONEY.

A... SHIP, YOU SAY?

AH...

MM...

MM... APPLES...

RIGHT, SO ABOUT SHIPPING...

WHAT IS IT?

GOTO

I... I WANT...

HM?

WELL SURE, WHY NOT?

THERE'S THERE'S

...APPLES...

KUU (RRR)

SHAGU

SHAGU

SHAGU (CRUNCH)

SHAGU

I WOULD'VE DONE WELL NOT TO GIVE HER A SILVER PIECE...

SHAGU

SHAGU

SHAGU

EARN YOUR OWN FOOD, WHY DON'T YOU.

ONE FOR ME...

IT'S AMUSING KNOWING WHAT SOMEONE ELSE IS THINKING.

YOU... MMPH... PRE- TENDED...

-BURP-

SHAGU

...LIKE YOU DIDN'T... ÷CHOMP÷ NOTICE!

SHAGU

HEY, I PAID FOR THEM.

MUSHA (MUNCH)

MINE!

バ

BASHI (SMACK)

DON'T LET ME STOP YOU. I'D PLANNED TO USE THAT MONEY FOR LODGING TONIGHT.

I'M HOLO THE WISEWOLF! I CAN MAKE THIS MUCH MONEY ANY TIME I WANT.

ゴク (GULP)

GOKU (GULP)

SFX: KOKURI (NOD)

ONCE YOU'RE DONE EATING, PLEASE.

MPH...

I WAS ...

KAHA (HACK)

か

SHAGU

I WASH...

NGU (NGHD)

ん

MMPH ...

SHAGU

BUT ...

SHAGU

SHOULDN'T A WISEWOLF BE ABLE TO CONQUER TEMPTATION?

AH HA HA!

YOU CERTAINLY ATE A LOT.

...WHEW!

APPLES ARE THE DEVIL'S FRUIT, FULL OF TEMPTING SWEETNESS AS THEY ARE.

I SEE...

WHILE ONE MAY LOSE MUCH BECAUSE OF AVARICE, NOTHING WAS EVER ACCOMPLISHED BY ABSTINENCE.

...AS YOU DO BUSINESS, I'LL JUST PUT A FEW WORDS IN TO HELP YOU BRING IN MORE PROFIT. AGREED?

I'VE NO MONEY AND NO IMMEDIATE MEANS TO EARN MONEY, SO...

OH, YES.

HM?

GOTO (CLUNK) ゴト
ゴト GOTO

SO, WHAT WAS THAT YOU WERE GOING TO SAY EARLIER?

......

WELL, I'LL TRY TO SAY SOMETHING TO BRING YOUR PROFIT UP, IF I CAN. WHATEVER THE DIF-FERENCE I MAKE, I KEEP.

YOU'LL SOON BE SELLING THE MARTEN FURS, YES?

PERHAPS AS SOON AS TODAY, YES.

IT'S DONE, THEN!

AGREED!

WHAT IS SHE THINK-ING...?

HOW MODEST OF YOU.

GOTO

GOTO

BUT THIS ISN'T A SURE THING. YOU'RE A MERCHANT, AFTER ALL— THERE MAY BE NO CHANCE FOR ME TO TALK UP OUR PRICE.

WISDOM IS KNOWING THYSELF FIRST.

WE'RE HERE TO SELL FURS. I WAS TOLD TO TALK TO THE PERSON ON THE LEFT.

IS HE A KNIGHT...?

WHERE ARE YOU HEADED?

HO THERE, SIR!

THIS WAY, IF YOU PLEASE.

RIGHT, THEN. I'LL JUST TAKE YOUR WAGON.

GOTO (THUNK)

GOTO

NO KID- DING.

HA HA HA!

A HORSE THAT COM- PLAINS— NOW THAT WOULD BE A SIGHT!

HE WORKS WITHOUT COMPLAINT; I'LL SAY THAT MUCH.

HO-HO! A GOOD HORSE, SIR! HE LOOKS STOUT OF HEART.

BURURU (NEIGH)

SFX: NADE (RUB) NADE

KARAN (CLANK)

KARAN

GU (YANK)

WELCOME, SIR!

KO (CLACK)

THEY'VE EXPANDED AGAIN...

KRAFT LAWRENCE, I PRESUME? WE THANK YOU FOR YOUR PATRONAGE.

KO

134

HE REMEMBERS MY NAME AFTER THREE YEARS? THAT'S A BIG COMPANY FOR YOU, I GUESS...

I'M TOLD YOU'VE COME TO SELL FURS TODAY.

INDEED I HAVE.

HO, THESE ARE GOOD MARTEN FURS INDEED.

SEVENTY FURS IN TOTAL.

'TIS A FINE LUSTER, TO BE SURE, AND WITH GOOD LIE. WHAT OF THEIR SIZE?

THEY WERE DRENCHED WITH RAIN ON THE WAY HERE, BUT LOOK... THEY'VE LOST NONE OF THEIR LUSTER.

YOU ONLY SEE FURS THIS FINE ONCE EVERY SEVERAL YEARS.

THE YEAR HAS BEEN A GOOD ONE FOR CROPS, SO MARTEN FUR IS SCARCE.

QUITE SO.

YOU'VE TRADED WHEAT WITH US IN THE PAST, SIR LAWRENCE?

KA (CLICK)

KA (CLICK)

YOU SAID YOU HAD SEVENTY?

OH, HO, THEY'RE NOT LACKING IN SIZE, EITHER.

ONE HUNDRED THIRTY-TWO SILVER TRENNI.

WHAT WOULD YOU SAY TO THIS?

WE CERTAINLY APPRECIATE YOUR BUSINESS.

I BROUGHT THEM TO YOU BECAUSE I'VE DONE BUSINESS WITH YOU IN THE PAST, BUT...

YOU DON'T SEE FURS LIKE THESE OFTEN.

AS WOULD WE, I ASSURE YOU.

GIVEN THAT...

FOR MY PART, I'D LIKE TO CONTINUE OUR ASSOCIA-TION.

PERFECT.

IN LIGHT OF FRIENDLY RELATIONS, THEN, WHAT SAY YOU TO ONE HUNDRED FORTY?

WHA—!

WAIT JUST A MOMENT!

は!! —BA— (WHAP)

UH...

ER... YES...

YES!

THAT'S WHAT YOU SAID?

ONE HUNDRED FORTY TRENNI, YES?

WHAT IS SHE ...?

チラ CHIRA (GLANCE)

ニ!! NI (GRIN)

AH, PERHAPS YOU DIDN'T NOTICE?

ズイ ZUI (ZIP)

...SO SURELY YOU PRETENDED NOT TO NOTICE? I CAN SEE I WON'T NEED TO HOLD BACK WITH YOU.

MM. I CAN SEE YOU'RE A FINE MERCHANT...

MY APOLOGIES, BUT HAVE I OVERLOOKED SOMETHING?

WHAT IS GOING ON HERE...?

I'M MERELY ASHAMED AT MY OWN IGNORANCE! IF YOU'LL KINDLY POINT OUT WHAT YOU'RE SPEAKING OF, WE WILL BE HAPPY TO ADJUST THE PRICE APPROPRIATELY.

BUN (SHAKE)

I...I MEANT NOTHING OF THE SORT!

BUN

ZUI (ZIP)

......

MASTER! IT'S NOT POLITE TO MAKE SPORT OF PEOPLE.

KURU (FWIP)

KURURI (TWIRL)

YES?

NOW, IF YOU PLEASE, SIR...

TH-THAT WAS CERTAINLY NOT MY AIM.

BUT PERHAPS YOU SHOULD BE THE ONE TO TELL HIM.

OR PERHAPS I SHOULD PUT IT THIS WAY—

YOU WON'T *SMELL* THEIR LIKE IN MANY YEARS.

YOU WON'T SEE THEIR LIKE IN MANY YEARS.

MM.

THESE ARE FINE FURS, AS YOU CAN SEE.

I QUITE AGREE.

TEE HEE HEE ラ ラ ラ ラ ラ HEE! HEE

'TIS A SCENT, BUT TO MISS IT YOU'D NEED TO BE BLIND!

GO RIGHT AHEAD.

WELL, A SNIFF IS WORTH A THOUSAND WORDS. WOULD YOU CARE TO SAMPLE THE SCENT?

SFX: KUN (SNIFF)

FRUIT INDEED.

ER, YES. IT SMELLS LIKE... FRUIT, I'D SAY.

AH...

OH? SMELL SOMETHING, DO YOU?

IT'S TRUE.

I SEE.

JUST AS FUR IS SCARCE THIS YEAR BECAUSE OF THE HARVEST, SO DID THE FOREST OVERFLOW WITH FRUIT.

DOES THE PROBLEM NOT COME, THEN, WHEN THE FUR IS MADE INTO CLOTHING, WHEN IT IS ACTUALLY USED?

WHILE A FUR'S LUSTER MIGHT BE BETTER OR WORSE, IT GENERALLY CHANGES LITTLE.

THIS MARTEN WAS SCAMPERING ABOUT IN THAT SAME FOREST UNTIL JUST A FEW DAYS AGO, AND IT ATE SO MUCH OF THAT PLENTIFUL FRUIT THAT THE SCENT SUFFUSED ITS BODY.

AS YOU CAN TELL, THIS PARTICULAR FUR HAS THE SWEET SCENT OF A MARTEN THAT HAS EATEN VERY WELL INDEED.

TRUE, AS YOU SAY.

GOOD FUR IS DURABLE; BAD FUR SOON WEARS THIN.

...

SFX: GU (STRETCH)

THERE'S NO WAY HE'LL PULL THAT HARD ON FUR HE'S NOT YET BOUGHT.

IT TOOK TWO STRONG MEN TO PULL THE HIDE CLEAR OF THE BODY, IT WAS SO TOUGH.

WHY, 'TWOULD SELL SO DEAR YOUR EYES WOULD POP OUT.

AND DON'T FORGET THE SCENT! IMAGINE COMING ACROSS A PERFUMED PIECE OF CLOTHING LIKE THIS AMONG COATS MADE FROM NOSE-WRINKLING MARTEN FUR.

THE FUR IS AS STRONG AS THE BEAST ITSELF WAS, AND WILL KEEP THE WEARER AS WARM AS A SPRING DAY, SHEDDING RAIN FROM DAWN 'TIL DUSK.

SO, WHAT DO YOU THINK WOULD BE A FAIR PRICE, THEN?

MMM...

HOW ABOUT THREE PIECES FOR EACH FUR, SO...

WHAT SAY YOU TO TWO HUNDRED TRENNI!?

SFX: KA (CLICK) KA

EH?

...210?

UH...

UH, NO! 210 PIECES, THEN!!

MASTER, PERHAPS WE SHOULD TRY ELSE- WHERE...

YOU HEARD THE MAN, MASTER.

HIKU CHIO

THE YOREND TAVERN

PUHAAAH!

AH, WINE!

MMMM!!

HAVE YOU EVER WORKED AS A MERCHANT?

WHAT TROUBLES YOU? AREN'T YOU GOING TO DRINK?

PORI (CMUNCH)

PORI

......

I DON'T KNOW HOW MANY DEALS YOU'VE DONE IN YOUR LIFE, BUT I WATCHED COUNTLESS TRANSACTIONS WHEN I WAS IN THE VILLAGE.

LONG AGO, I SAW A VERY CLEVER MAN USE THAT TECHNIQUE.

OH, THAT? I DIDN'T THINK OF IT MY-SELF.

EH?

......

IN THE END, THE CREDIT IS MINE, THOUGH!

THOUGH THE APPLES ARE DUE SOME THANKS AS WELL, FOR HAVING THEIR SCENT RUB OFF AFTER ONLY HALF A DAY!

144

...YOU MAY HAVE A POINT.

I WON'T SAY IT'S HIS OWN FAULT FOR BEING TRICKED, BUT HE'LL BE IMPRESSED ONCE HE FIGURES IT OUT.

A REAL MERCHANT KNOWS TO BE IMPRESSED.

THERE'S NO POINT IN BEING ANGRY WHEN YOU'VE BEEN TRICKED.

AND THIS WIZENED OLD TRADER THINKS YOU'RE JUST A BABE IN ARMS!

MMPH!

BORI (CRUNCH)

BORI

THAT'S QUITE A SERMON. YOU SOUND LIKE A WIZENED OLD TRADER.

PORI

GUI (TOSS)

HA HA HA HA HA HA HA HA

ALL THIS ASIDE, DID YOU DO AS YOU WERE SUPPOSED TO?

I WONDER WHEN ZHEREN WILL APPEAR...

BUT THEY DIDN'T SEEM TO BE HIDING ANYTHING.

YES, I ASKED AROUND THE MILONE COMPANY TO SEE IF ANYBODY KNEW ABOUT NATIONS THAT WOULD BE ISSUING NEW SILVER CURRENCY.

THAT'S WHY WE'RE IN-VOL-VED.

BUT CHANCES FOR THIS KIND OF DEAL AREN'T COMMON.

HM...

MAKES FOR GOOD BUSINESS RELATIONS.

AS LONG AS THE INFORMATION ISN'T SOMETHING THAT NEEDS TO BE MONO-POLIZED, THEY'LL NORMALLY SHARE IT.

WHATEVER THE TRICK IS, AS LONG AS I FIGURE IT OUT AND COME OUT AHEAD, THAT'S ALL THAT MATTERS THAT'S THE GOAL.

AFTER THAT, WE MET WITH ZHEREN AND TALKED OF THE CONTRACT.

IT WAS A CONSERVATIVE SHARE, BUT IN THE CASE OF A LOSS, HE WOULD OWE ONLY THE INFORMATION FEE, AND NO MORE.

ZHEREN'S DUE WAS TO BE TEN TRENNI FOR THE INFORMATION, PLUS TEN PERCENT OF THE PROFIT.

THE NEXT DAY, WE SIGNED THE CONTRACT BEFORE A PUBLIC WITNESS.

WE WOULD SETTLE UP ABOUT SIX MONTHS HENCE, THREE DAYS BEFORE THE SPRING MARKET. THAT WOULD BE ENOUGH TIME FOR THE MARKETS TO REFLECT THE CHANGE IN CURRENCY.

AND THAT AFTERNOON ...

DON'T PLAY WITH COIN.

THIS IS THE SILVER THE BOY MENTIONED, YES?

KORO CSPIN

KORO

AND ALSO SIMPLY BECAUSE THIS TOWN WAS WITHIN THE NATION OF TRENNI.

THIS WAS BECAUSE, AMONG THE HUNDREDS OF DIFFERENT KINDS OF COIN IN THE WORLD, IT WAS ONE OF THE MOST TRUSTED.

TRENNI SILVER WAS THE MOST WIDELY-USED CURRENCY IN THE REGION.

TRUST IN THE COIN'S VALUE IS CRUCIAL.

THERE ARE HUNDREDS OF CURRENCIES IN THE WORLD, AND THE AMOUNT OF GOLD OR SILVER IN EACH VARIES CONSTANTLY.

IT'S A WELL-TRUSTED COIN IN THIS REGION.

JUST WHAT ERA IS SHE TALKING ABOUT...?

IT USED TO BE THAT TRADE WAS CONDUCTED IN ANIMAL SKINS.

HUH. I ONLY KNEW OF A FEW DIFFERENT KINDS OF MONEY.

TRUST-ED?

148

FOR EXAMPLE?

WELL, THERE ARE SEVERAL POSSI-BILITES.

SO, HOW ABOUT IT? HAVE YOU WORKED SOMETHING OUT NOW THAT YOU KNOW WHICH COIN HE WAS TALKING ABOUT?

GOTO
GORO (ROLL)
GOTO (THUNK)

I DON'T WANT ANY TROUBLE.

AND GIVE ME THE CHANGE.

HEY, DON'T RUN INTO PEOPLE WALKING IN THE STREET.

WASA

WASA (SHUFFLE)

?

......

IT'S HARD TO SEE YOU AS ANYTHING ELSE WHEN YOUR MOUTH IS STICKY WITH HONEY.

DON'T TREAT ME LIKE A PUP, THEN.

BAFU

BAFU (CHOMP)

YOU CERTAINLY CAN'T TAKE A JOKE.

ばし BASHI (WHAP)

AM I CUTE?

I'M A VERY SERIOUS PERSON.

OH, RIGHT, RIGHT.

SO... WHAT WAS IT YOU WERE THINKING ABOUT?

IT'S GOT A RESPECTABLE SILVER CONTENT AND IS QUITE POPULAR IN THE MARKET-PLACE. YOU COULD SAY IT'S THE TRENNI'S RIVAL.

SO... HERE, TAKE THIS COIN, A SILVER FIRIN. IT'S FROM A NATION THREE RIVERS SOUTH OF HERE.

THERE ARE REASONS TO RAISE THE SILVER CONTENT.

SO, BACK TO THE TRENNI COIN. ZHEREN MAY WELL BE TELLING THE TRUTH.

OH?

HUH. SEEMS SOME THINGS NEVER CHANGE: A NATION'S POWER IS IN ITS MONEY.

GAFU

GAFU (MUNCH)

ALL THE FOREIGN KING NEEDS TO DO IS CUT OFF YOUR SUPPLY OF MONEY, AND YOUR MARKETPLACE WILL DIE.

IF YOUR NATION'S CURRENCY IS OVERWHELMED BY A FOREIGN COIN, YOU'VE BEEN JUST AS THOROUGHLY CONQUERED.

NATIONS DO NOT ALWAYS FIGHT THROUGH STRENGTH OF ARMS.

WELL, I SUPPOSE MY EARS AREN'T COMPLETELY FOOLPROOF.

SO THEY'RE INCREASING THE SILVER CONTENT IN ORDER TO GAIN ADVANTAGE OVER THEIR RIVAL.

PERO (LICK)

THEY CONTROL YOUR ECONOMY.

WITHOUT MONEY, YOU CAN NEITHER BUY NOR SELL.

I QUITE AGREE.

MM.

IT'S ENTIRELY POSSIBLE THAT ZHEREN WASN'T ACTUALLY LYING.

WELL, EITHER WAY IS A POSSIBILITY!

WELL, I MIGHT BE ANGRY AT THAT!

I SURELY DID.

WHAT, DID YOU THINK I WAS GOING TO BE ANGRY?

SFX: BU (SPIT)

SO, TO THE MINT?

NOW THAT WE KNOW WHICH COIN TO LOOK INTO, WE'RE GOING TO LOOK INTO IT.

SO WHERE ARE WE GOING NOW?

ONCE WE'RE THERE, WE'LL SEE HOW THE COIN'S BEEN DOING RECENTLY.

IF A MERCHANT LIKE ME SHOWED UP AT THE MINT, THE ONLY GREETING I'D GET WOULD BE THE BUSINESS END OF A SPEAR. NO, WE'RE GOING TO SEE THE CAMBIST.

HUH. I GUESS THERE ARE THINGS EVEN I DON'T KNOW.

PUU (POUT)

SPICE & WOLF

A CANAL DIVERGES FROM THE RIVER SLAUDE AND THROUGH THE CENTER OF PAZZIO.

CAMBISTS AND GOLD-SMITHS HAVE LONG DONE BUSINESS ON BRIDGES.

WITH THE SLUICE GATES CLOSED, FLOODING WAS IMPOSSIBLE, SO BUSINESS COULD BE SAFELY CONDUCTED ON THE HUGE BRIDGE THAT CONNECTED BOTH SIDES OF THE CANAL.

WHAT DO YOU MEAN, "SEE"?

MM.

SO WE'LL SEE HOW THE COIN'S BEEN DOING RECENTLY.

BEFORE A CURRENCY'S VALUE CHANGES DRASTI- CALLY...

...THERE ARE ALWAYS SIGNS.

MMM...

SOMETHING LIKE THAT. WHEN THE PURITY IS GOING TO INCREASE A LOT, IT INCREASES A LITTLE AT A TIME, AND THE SAME IS TRUE WHEN IT DROPS.

HA HA HA!

LIKE THE WEATHER BEFORE A STORM?

SINCE WHAT YOU'RE ACTUALLY DOING IS ARBITRARILY ASSIGNING A VALUE TO SOMETHING WITH NO INHERENT WORTH, YOU CAN THINK OF IT AS A BALL OF TRUST.

RELATIVE TO THE ABSOLUTE VALUE OF THE GOLD OR SILVER IN THEM, COINS ARE OBVIOUSLY MORE HIGHLY VALUED.

ADDITIONALLY, EVEN A CAMBIST CANNOT ALWAYS DETECT CHANGES IN A COIN'S PURITY.

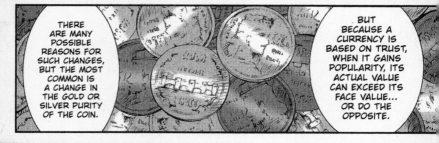

THERE ARE MANY POSSIBLE REASONS FOR SUCH CHANGES, BUT THE MOST COMMON IS A CHANGE IN THE GOLD OR SILVER PURITY OF THE COIN.

BUT BECAUSE A CURRENCY IS BASED ON TRUST, WHEN IT GAINS POPULARITY, ITS ACTUAL VALUE CAN EXCEED ITS FACE VALUE... OR DO THE OPPOSITE.

THAT'S WHY PEOPLE ARE SO SENSITIVE TO CHANGES IN A CURRENCY... EVEN CHANGES TOO SMALL TO DETECT WITH EYEGLASSES OR A SCALE CAN STILL BE CONSIDERED MAJOR.

......

SO, THAT MEANS...

HMPH.

MAYBE THAT WAS TOO MUCH.

...WHEN THE COIN ISSUER WANTS TO CHANGE THE PURITY, FIRST THEY'LL MAKE A MINUTE CHANGE...

...THEN ADJUST IT UP OR DOWN BASED ON THE MARKET REACTION, YES?

SHE UNDERSTOOD SO QUICKLY...

NORMALLY THAT TAKES ABOUT A MONTH TO UNDERSTAND...

Y-YEAH, THAT'S ABOUT RIGHT.

THE HUMAN WORLD CERTAINLY IS COMPLICATED.

THERE ARE SO MANY; HOW DOES ONE CHOOSE?

SFX: KYORO (GLANCE) KYORO

ANY MERCHANT WORTH HIS SALT HAS A FAVORITE CAMBIST IN EACH TOWN.

FOLLOW ME!

HO, WEIZ! IT'S BEEN A WHILE!

AH...

THERE HE IS.

SO, WHAT BRINGS YOU HERE TODAY? YOU'VE NEED OF MY SERVICES, EH?

I GUESS YOU'RE DOING ALL RIGHT FOR YOURSELF AS A CAMBIST!

HA HA HA HA!

FUWA (FLUTTER)

!?

HUH... WAIT, PICKED HER UP, YOU SAY!?

PICKED HER UP IN PASLOE ON MY WAY HERE.

WHO'S THE GIRL!?

BA (WHAM)

KYORO (GLANCE)

MM? MM... MIGHT NOT BE QUITE THE WORD FOR IT, BUT MORE OR LESS, I'LL ALLOW.

WELL, MORE OR LESS. WOULDN'T YOU SAY?

KYORO

159

HMPH, FINE THEN. WHAT DO YOU WANT?

I'VE COME FOR A FAVOR.

WEIZ, CAN YOU DO THAT LATER?

A RECENTLY ISSUED TRENNI COIN?

THAT'S RIGHT. IF YOU CAN, I'D LIKE THE THREE MOST RECENT VERSIONS.

WELL, WATCH YOURSELF, FRIEND. 'TISN'T EASY TO GET AHEAD OF THE CROWD.

SOMETHING LIKE THAT.

WHAT, DO YOU KNOW SOMETHING ABOUT THE PURITY CHANGING?

...HERE IT IS.

THEN THE ONE BEFORE THAT...

THE MOST RECENT ONE CAME OUT JUST LAST MONTH, AT ADVENT.

WE HANDLE MONEY ALL DAY AND HAVEN'T NOTICED ANYTHING. THEY'RE CAST IN THE SAME MOLD, USING THE SAME INGREDIENTS.

THERE'S NO REASON TO CHANGE THE COIN.

THE LINEUP OF ARTISANS AT THE MINT HASN'T CHANGED IN YEARS, AND THERE'VE BEEN NO COUPS.

HM. WHAT NOW, I WONDER.

IT'S NO USE, FRIEND. IF YOU COULD TELL JUST BY LOOKING, WE'D HAVE NOTICED LONG AGO.

CHARI (CLINK)

LET ME SEE THEM.

DON'T WANT TO MELT THEM DOWN, EH?

DON'T BE RIDICULOUS, I'D GO STRAIGHT TO JAIL.

PON (PAT)

PON

HAAAAA
(GAAASP)

NIKO
(SMILE)

KYUUUU
(SQUEEEZE)

KYU
(CLASP)

OH, CERTAINLY, CERTAINLY.

OH, SIR, YOU'RE SUCH A CAD!

CAN YOU TELL ANYTHING, HOLO, MY DEAR?

KOTO (THUD)

KACHI KACHI (CLINK)

I CANNOT.

OH, NO! YOU'RE RIGHT!

UH, WEIZ? YOUR JOB...?

GOSH, I WISH YOU COULD STAY AND TALK MORE...

OH, TOO BAD! TOO BAD INDEED!

SO, WHAT ABOUT THE SILVER PURITY? HAS IT RISEN OR FALLEN?

I'M THE ONLY ONE WHO KNOWS ABOUT THOSE EARS OF YOURS, AFTER ALL.

YOU'VE GOTTEN QUITE GOOD AT FERRETING THE TRUTH OUT, HAVEN'T YOU?

I KNOW I SAW THEM TWITCH.

YOUR LIE WAS UN-EXPECTED.

BUT WHAT SURPRISED ME WAS THAT YOU DIDN'T SAY ANYTHING ABOUT IT BACK THERE.

CAN'T LET MY GUARD DOWN.

COMPENSATION?

I SUPPOSE YOU CAN CONSIDER IT COMPENSATION.

...WE DON'T KNOW WHAT OTHER PEOPLE NEARBY WOULD'VE DONE. THE FEWER PEOPLE AS KNOW A SECRET, THE BETTER, NO?

WHETHER OR NOT HE WOULD'VE BELIEVED ME, ASIDE...

YOU WERE A BIT JEALOUS BACK THEN, NO?

ZUI CLEAND

169

OH, DON'T WORRY ABOUT IT. ALL MEN BURN WITH FOOLISH JEALOUSY.

BUT WOMEN ARE FOOLS TO TAKE DELIGHT IN IT.

COM-PEN-SATION FOR THAT.

ZUI (LEAN)

YET HERE YOU ARE, IN HUMAN FORM. BEST NOT BARE YOUR FANGS NOW, IN FRONT OF YOUR BELOVED WOLVES!

THOUGH TO ME, YOU'RE BOTH JUST LOWLY HUMANS.

THIS WORLD IS FULL OF FOOLS, THAT'S CERTAIN!

SU (SIT)

KU FU FU!

JOKING ASIDE, THOUGH ...

HAH, A FLICK OF MY LOVELY TAIL CHARMS HUMAN AND WOLF ALIKE!

IT WAS JUST A BIT, BUT THE NEW COINS HAVE A SLIGHTLY DULLER SOUND.

SFX: TON (TAP) TON

HMM...BUT IF THAT'S TRUE, IT'S REASONABLE TO ASSUME THAT ZHEREN WAS LYING ALL ALONG.

A DULLER SOUND MEANT THAT THE SILVER PURITY HAD DROPPED. IT COULD BE A SIGN THAT THE TRENNI WAS GOING TO BECOME LESS PURE.

DULLER?

'TIS A PUZZLE-MENT.

BUT IF HE'D WANTED TO SWINDLE THE INFORMATION FEE, HE COULD'VE JUST DONE IT AT THE CHURCH.

WELL, ZHEREN BROUGHT ME THE DEAL, SO HE MUST HAVE SOMETHING TO GAIN FROM IT.

YOU SELL AT THE HIGH PRICE AND BUY IT BACK UP AT THE LOW, POCKETING THE DIFFERENCE. BUT HALF A YEAR ISN'T ENOUGH TIME FOR THAT.

THE ONLY WAY TO PROFIT FROM A DROP IN SILVER PURITY IS A LONG-TERM INVESTMENT.

I THOUGHT IF I COULD ASCERTAIN THE STATE OF THE SILVER COIN, I'D UNDERSTAND HIS MOTIVATION, BUT IT DOESN'T ADD UP.

171

BUT IF HE'S NOT RESPONSIBLE FOR LOSSES...

ASSUMING HE'S NOT SOME KIND OF FOOL.

HE MUST.

CHIRA (GLANCE)

IS IT COMMON FOR THE SILVER PURITY TO DROP SLIGHTLY?

WHAT?

PFFT!

HM. AND YET OUT OF NOWHERE, HERE'S A DEAL THAT HINGES ON THE PURITY OF SILVER COIN.

NO, NORMALLY THE PURITY IS CONTROLLED WITH EXTREME CARE.

NOW, YOU BEING IN THAT VILLAGE, AT THAT TIME, WITH THAT SHEAF OF WHEAT...THAT WAS CHANCE. THERE IS NOTHING SO HARD AS TELLING CHANCE FROM FATE.

THAT IS A STRANGE EXAMPLE.

IT'S HARDER THAN ROMANCE FOR A SHUT-IN!

URK!

IS THAT JUST CHANCE?

YOU'RE LOST IN YOUR OWN THOUGHTS.

WHEN I'M HUNTING, SOMETIMES I'LL CLIMB A TREE. THE FOREST LOOKS DIFFERENT FROM ON HIGH.

WHEN THAT HAPPENS, YOU NEED A NEW PERSPECTIVE.

WHAT IF THE PERSON PLANNING SOMETHING ISN'T THAT LAD?

FOR EXAMPLE...

HE MIGHT HAVE BEEN HIRED BY SOMEBODY ELSE, AND THOSE WAGES MOTIVATED HIM TO PULL YOU INTO THIS STRANGE DEAL.

THERE'S NO REASON ZHEREN'S PROFIT HAS TO COME FROM YOU.

SO... HAVE YOU SEEN ANYTHING NEW?

IF ZHEREN HAD BEEN HIRED BY SOMEONE ELSE TO BUY UP SILVER COIN...

IF ZHEREN'S GAINS WERE NOT COMING FROM LAWRENCE, BUT FROM SOME OTHER PARTY!...

THE MASSIVE SCALE OF THE PLAN COULD YIELD OBSCENE PROFITS.

I CAN ONLY THINK OF ONE EXPLANATION THAT FITS THE FACTS.

HEH. YOU'VE FIGURED SOMETHING OUT, HAVE YOU?

LET'S GO.

WHERE?

HM?

UH...

BA (WHAM)

To be continued in Volume 2...

STAFF
KOUMEKEITO
TOITENTSU
S.T
YAKKUN

THANKS

VOLUME 1 OF THE SPICE AND WOLF MANGA IS FINALLY, FINALLY ON SALE. IN THE YEAR OR SO THAT IT'S BEEN IN PROGRESS, I'VE HAD THE SUPPORT OF MANY, MANY PEOPLE. THANK YOU SO MUCH. TO THE AUTHOR, ISUNA HASEKURA, THE ILLUSTRATOR JYUU AYAKURA, AND MY VARIOUS EDITORS AND ILLUSTRATION STAFF, AND ESPECIALLY TO ALL THE FANS OF SPICE AND WOLF, I WANT TO EXTEND MY DEEPEST AND MOST HEARTFELT THANKS. I'LL DO MY BEST AS WE HEAD INTO THE SECOND VOLUME!

KEITO KOUME
2008. 3

IT'S HUGE!

■ WHEN RESEARCHING MEDIEVAL HISTORY, I LEARNED ALL SORTS OF INTERESTING THINGS. FOR EXAMPLE, THE VARIOUS KINDS OF IMPLEMENTS THAT WERE CARVED FROM ANIMAL HORN. HORN WAS THE PLASTIC OF THE MIDDLE AGES, AND IT WAS USED FOR EVERYTHING FROM SPOONS TO WINDOW GLASS!

IN THE MEDIEVAL DAYS, EVERYONE HAD THEIR OWN PERSONAL SPOON, APPARENTLY. (ALTHOUGH GENERALLY THEY JUST ATE WITH THEIR HANDS, I GUESS.)

DO YOU SUPPOSE HOLO GOT LAWRENCE TO BUY HER HER OWN SPOON?

BASA (SWISH)

BASA

SPICE & WOLF

● HOORAY! THE FIRST VOLUME OF MANGA! I CAN'T HIDE MY SURPRISE AT HOW QUICKLY IT'S COME TO PUBLICATION, BUT MOST IMPRESSIVE OF ALL IS THE INCREDIBLE QUALITY OF MR. KOUME'S ARTWORK!
ISUNA HASEKURA

■ CONGRATULATIONS ON THE FIRST MANGA VOLUME! MR. KOUME'S VERSION OF HOLO IS JUST ADORABLE, AND ALWAYS GETTING THE BETTER OF EVERYBODY! I LOOK FORWARD TO SEEING MORE.
JYUU AYAKURA

SPICE & WOLF ❶

Isuna Hasekura
Keito Koume
Character design:
Jyuu Ayakura

Translation: Paul Starr

Lettering: Alexis Eckerman

OOKAMI TO KOUSHINRYOU Vol. 1
©Isuna Hasekura/Keito Koume 2008
Edited by ASCII MEDIA WORKS
First published in Japan in 2008 by
KADOKAWA CORPORATION, Tokyo.
English translation rights arranged with
KADOKAWA CORPORATION, Tokyo,
through Tuttle-Mori Agency, Inc., Tokyo.

English translation © 2010 by Yen Press, LLC

Yen Press
1290 Avenue of the Americas
New York, NY 10104

Visit us at YENPRESS.COM
FACEBOOK.COM/YENPRESS
TWITTER.COM/YENPRESS
YENPRESS.TUMBLR.COM
INSTAGRAM.COM/YENPRESS

First Yen Press Edition: April 2010

Yen Press is an imprint of Yen Press, LLC.
The Yen Press name and logo are trademarks of Yen Press, LLC.

Library of Congress Control Number: 2015956856

ISBN: 978-0-316-07339-4

24 23 22 21 20 19 18 17 16 15

BVG

Printed in the United States of America

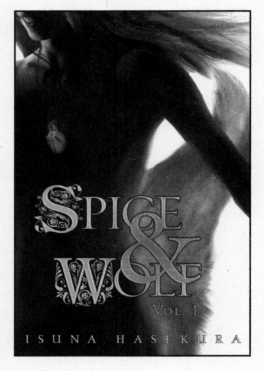

MAYBE THAT IS WHY THERE IS NO NEED FOR THEM...

...TO HONOR THE ANCIENT AGREEMENT, SHE THOUGHT.

IN ANY CASE...

...SHE KNEW SHE NO LONGER HAD A PLACE HERE.

THE VILLAGERS WHO TENDED THE WHEAT AS THE YEARS PASSED...

...LIVED FOR SEVENTY YEARS AT THE MOST.

LATELY, IT WAS A POPULAR SORT OF EXPRESSION, AND THERE WERE FEW REMAINING...

...WHO WIELDED IT WITH THE SORT OF FAMILIARITY OR AWE...

...IT HAD HELD IN THE PAST.

WHEN THE HARVEST IS POOR...

...IT IS SAID THAT THE WOLF HAS EATEN IT.

WHEN THE WIND IS TOO STRONG, AND THE STALKS ARE BLOWN OVER...

...IT IS SAID THAT THE WOLF HAS TRAMPLED THEM.

IN THIS VILLAGE...

...WHEN THE RIPENED EARS OF WHEAT SWAY IN THE BREEZE...

...IT IS SAID THAT A WOLF RUNS THROUGH THEM.

SPICE&WOLF

CONTENTS

Trenni Silver

The most common currency in the Pazzio area, it is regarded as being reliably pure in silver. The individual pictured on the coin above is the 11th king of the Trenni dynasty.

Introduction

The Church's influence is waning, and the time when all in the land prostrated themselves before its authority has passed.

Lawrence, who dreams of one day opening his own shop in a town somewhere, is driving his wagon—piled high with marten furs—to the village of Pasloe. He makes camp at the outskirts of the village, which is holding a festival in honor of the wolf-god of the harvest, when a strange thing happens...

Map Illustration: Hidetada Idemitsu

Kingdom of Winfiel

Gerube

Dolan Plains

Mt. Roef

Roef River

Nyohhira

Yoitsu

Ploania

Lenos

Roam River

Teleo

Emberch

Kumersun

Lamtra

Ruvinheigen

Poroson

Pazzio

Slaud River

Pasloe

Yorenz

N
W E
S

Lawrence

A traveling merchant in the seventh year of his career, age 25. He is quite clever, but as a merchant, there are still many areas he knows little about.

Holo

Introducing herself as the God of the Harvest for the village of Pasloe, this strange girl has wolf ears and a tail.

Zheren

A novice merchant who is staying at the church. He proposes a peculiar deal to Lawrence.

Weiz

A cambist working at the bridge in the port town of Pazzio, and a good friend of Lawrence's.

Yarei

A peasant of the village of Pasloe. He was the village's agent in the days when Lawrence traded wheat.

SPICE & WOLF